2.02
945s
2010

OCT 1 4 2010

D1295523

Fierce Fighters
SAMURAI

Charlotte Guillain

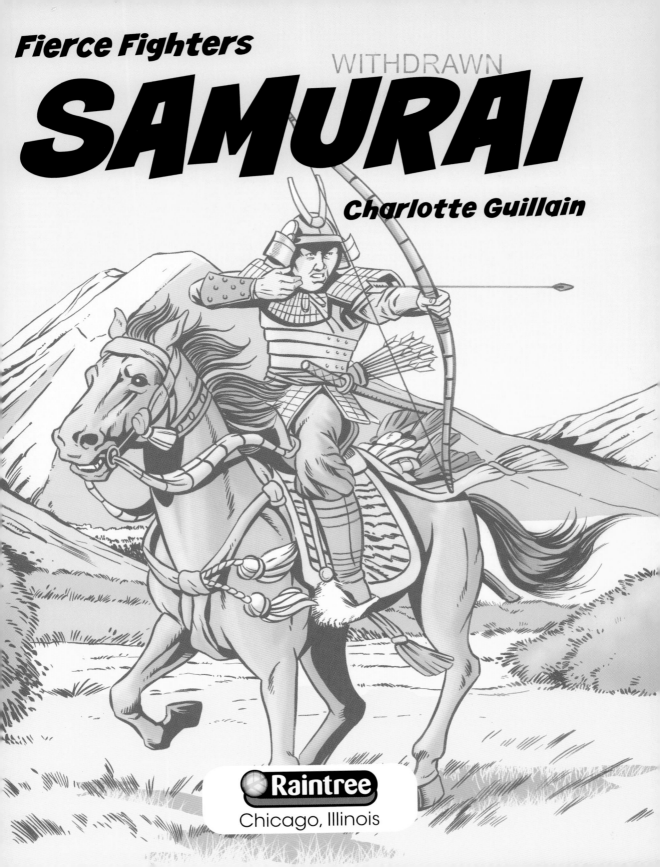

Raintree
Chicago, Illinois

www.heinemannraintree.com
Visit our website to find out
more information about
Heinemann-Raintree books.

To order:
☎ Phone 888-454-2279
🖥 Visit www.heinemannraintree.com
to browse our catalog and order online.

©2010 Raintree
an imprint of Capstone Global Library, LLC
Chicago, Illinois

All rights reserved. No part of this publication may be
reproduced or transmitted in any form or by any means,
electronic or mechanical, including photocopying,
recording, taping, or any information storage and
retrieval system, without permission in writing from the
publisher.

Edited by Rebecca Rissman, Nancy Dickmann,
and Catherine Veitch
Designed by Joanna Hinton-Malivoire
Original illustrations © Capstone Global Library 2010
Original illustrations by Miracle Studios
Picture research by Tracy Cummins
Production by Victoria Fitzgerald
Originated by Capstone Global Library
Printed and bound in China by Leo Paper Products Ltd

14 13 12 11 10
10 9 8 7 6 5 4 3 2 1

**Library of Congress Cataloging-in-
Publication Data**
Guillain, Charlotte.
  Samurai / Charlotte Guillain.
    p. cm. -- (Fierce fighters)
  Includes bibliographical references and index.
  ISBN 978-1-4109-3765-0 (hc) -- ISBN 978-1-4109-
3773-5 (pbk.) 1. Samurai--Juvenile literature. I. Title.
  DS827.S3G85 2010
  355.00952--dc22
                              2009030858

Acknowledgments
The Bridgeman Art Library International p. **15** (© Look
and Learn); akg-images p. **16**; Alamy pp. **17** (© Jon
Bower London), **23** (© JTB Photo Communications, Inc),
CORBIS pp. **21** (© Michael Maslan Historic Photographs),
22 (© Asian Art & Archaeology, Inc.); Getty Images pp. **7**
(Erik Von Weber), **11** (Tohoku Color Agency), **19** (Felice
Beato), **24** (ime & Life Pictures); Heinemann Raintree
pp. 28 top (Karon Dubke), **28 bottom** (Karon Dubke),
29 top (Karon Dubke), **29 bottom** (Karon Dubke);
Photolibrary p. **10** (Radius Images); Shutterstock pp. **18**
(© Anatoliy Samara), **26** (© Jose Gil); The Art Archive pp.
12 (Bibliothèque des Arts Décoratifs Paris / Gianni Dagli
Orti), **14** (Bibliothèque des Arts Décoratifs Paris / Gianni
Dagli Orti); THE Kobal Collection p. **27** (WARNER BROS. /
JAMES, DAVID).

Front cover illustration of a samurai warrior reproduced
with permission of Miracle Studios.

The publishers would like to thank Jane Penrose for her
assistance in the preparation of this book.

Every effort has been made to contact copyright holders
of material reproduced in this book. Any omissions will be
rectified in subsequent printings if notice is given to the
publishers.

All the internet addresses (URLs) given in this book were
valid at the time of going to press. However, due to the
dynamic nature of the Internet, some addresses may have
changed or ceased to exist since publication. While the
author and publishers regret any inconvenience this may
cause readers, no responsibility for any such changes can
be accepted by either the author or the publishers.

Some words are shown in bold, **like this.** You can find
out what they mean by looking in the glossary.

Contents

Two rulers are at war. Samurai run into battle to fight for their masters. These fierce **warriors** are afraid of nothing, not even death. Their weapons are deadly, and their masks look like devils.

Surrender now or die fighting the samurai!

Samurai timeline

1500s	The samurai fight in many Japanese wars
1600s	Japan is peaceful
1800s	The samurai are banned in Japan
1900s	Japan fights in World War Two
2000s	You are reading this book

Who Were the Samurai?

The samurai were special **warriors** who lived in Japan. They were like knights. Rulers **hired**, or paid, samurai to fight in wars.

Where the Samurai lived

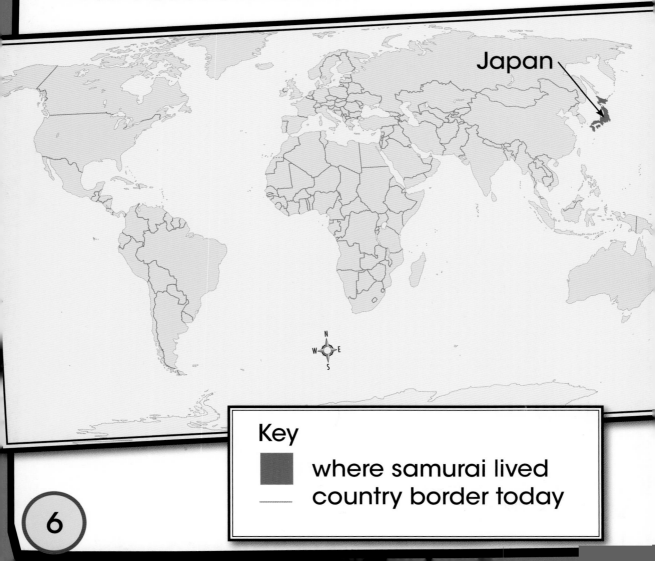

Japan

Key

■ where samurai lived
— country border today

DID YOU KNOW?

Samurai means "those who serve."

Becoming a Samurai

Only men from special families could be samurai. They started training when they were small children. They learned to fight with wooden swords. Later they learned to ride horses, shoot a bow and arrow, throw a **spear**, and fight.

The samurai had to learn how to use many different weapons.

DID YOU KNOW?

Samurai had to learn how to shoot a bow and arrow while riding a horse. It was not easy!

9

Samurai **warriors** learned **tactics**, or ways of fighting, that would help them win battles. But the most important samurai training was learning to use a curved sword with deadly skill.

Samurai practiced many of the martial arts people still learn today.

DID YOU KNOW?

Young samurai also studied poetry and learned how to behave well.

Samurai Rules

Most samurai **warriors** would only fight for one master. When his master was killed or **insulted**, a samurai had to find his master's enemy and kill him.

DID YOU KNOW?

Ronin were samurai who had no master. They would fight for anyone who paid them.

If a samurai **warrior** lost a battle, then he would often kill himself. This was called *seppuku* (say *seh-poo-koo*). The samurai would take his sword and cut his own stomach open. He would rather die like this than be a **prisoner**.

DID YOU KNOW?

When a samurai did *seppuku,* a friend would often cut off his head to finish the job quickly.

Samurai Weapons

Samurai **warriors** wore a special suit of **armor**. Some samurai decorated their helmets with evil-looking masks to scare their enemies.

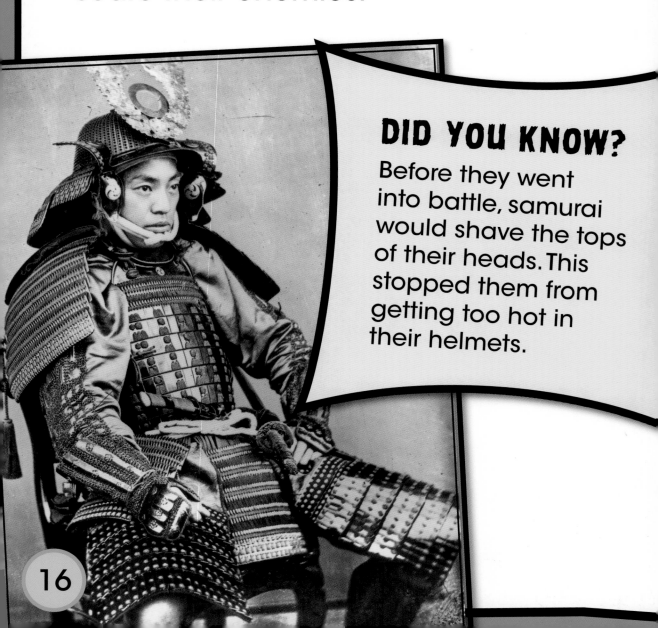

DID YOU KNOW?
Before they went into battle, samurai would shave the tops of their heads. This stopped them from getting too hot in their helmets.

The most important weapon for a samurai **warrior** was his sword. Their curved swords were strong and had a sharp **blade**, or edge. They could cut a person in half with one slice. Samurai also had a shorter straight sword.

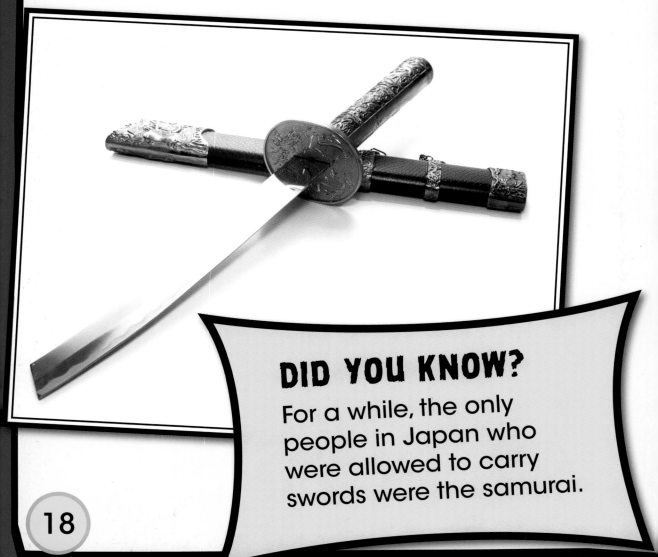

DID YOU KNOW?

For a while, the only people in Japan who were allowed to carry swords were the samurai.

Samurai **warriors** also used a *naginata*. This was a long pole with a sharp, curved **blade**. Women samurai liked to use this weapon. They spun the naginata to stop their enemies from getting too close. Then they stabbed them with the blade.

naginata

DID YOU KNOW?

When guns arrived in Japan, the samurai used them, too. But they would always choose to use their swords first.

Famous Samurai Warriors

Sanada Yukimura was called the "number one **warrior** in Japan." But when he was beaten after a long battle, he knew he must die. Sanada took off his helmet, and the enemy cut off his head with one slice.

Sanada Yukimura

Uesugi Kenshin

DID YOU KNOW?

Some stories about the great warrior Uesugi Kenshin say he was killed by a samurai warrior as he used the toilet!

Samurai Women

Samurai families taught young girls **martial arts**. Girls also learned how to use weapons. Women did not usually fight in battle, but they often had to keep their homes safe from attackers.

DID YOU KNOW?

One samurai story is about a woman **warrior** called Tomoe Gozen. She fought with her husband in many battles.

The End of the Samurai

After many years people in Japan stopped fighting. A ruler took over who **banned** samurai **warriors**. They were not allowed to wear their swords. Today the only samurai left are in films and cartoons.

DID YOU KNOW?

Many of today's **martial arts**, such as karate, kendo, and judo have changed very little since the samurai.

Samurai Activity

Each samurai warrior had a personal flag, called a *sashimono*. He carried the flag on his back into battle.

Make your own sashimono

You will need:
- card
- small piece of cane
- string
- paints
- paint brushes
- scissors

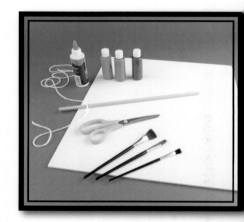

1. Cut out a card rectangle about 12 in by 16 in. Paint a design on the card. You could ask an adult to help you look up pictures of flags real samurai used.

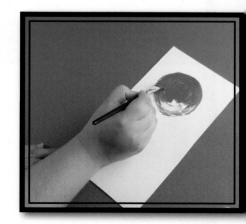

2. When the paint is dry, make holes along one side of your flag. Use string to tie the flag to the piece of cane.

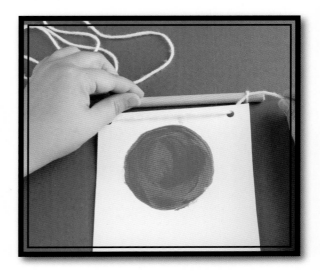

You are ready to march into battle!

Glossary

armor covering made of metal or leather to protect a soldier

banned not allowed

blade flat, cutting part of a knife or sword

hire pay for a service or use

insulted said something rude about someone

martial arts traditional training of body and mind

prisoner person kept in a jail or prison

spear weapon with sharp point on a long pole

tactic way of doing something, such as fighting, to get results that are wanted

warrior fighter

Find Out More

Books

Kalman, Bobbie. *Japan: The Culture*. New York City: Crabtree, 2008.

Leavitt, Caroline. *Samurai*. Mankato, Minn.: Capstone Edge Books, 2007.

Powell, Jillian. *Looking at Japan*. Strongsville, OH: Gareth Stevens, 2007.

Websites

http://samuraikids.com.au/books.html
This website teaches all about the samurai and introduces kids to samurai kid characters.

http://web-japan.org/kidsweb/index.html
This website tells all about the history of Japan.

Find out

Can you find out about Japan today?

31

Index